ABC's IN THE KITCHEN

A Cookbook for Kids

Cooking through the alphabet with you and your child!

by Megan E. Barney and Catherine E. Montenegro

Published by Eagen Montenegro

Paperback 978-1-7344238-0-8
Hardback 978-1-7344238-1-5
Ebook 978-1-7344238-2-2

ABC's in the Kitchen: A Cookbook for Kids
© 2020 Megan E. Barney and Catherine E. Montenegro.
All rights reserved. No part of this publication may be reproduced,
stored in a retrieval system, or transmitted, in any form,
or by any means, electronic, mechanical, photocopying, recording,
or otherwise, without the prior consent of the publisher.

About the Authors

Catherine, a literacy consulting teacher, has been an educator for over 40 years. The American Library Association, in their Year Book, published a reading program she wrote that was implemented in many schools in Long Beach, California. She is Reading Recovery credentialed and was a keynote speaker at many major reading conferences. One of her most gratifying accomplishments, was being selected "Teacher of the Year" for the Long Beach School District. Catherine lives in Southern California with her husband of over 50 years. She has two married daughters and is Nana to four grandchildren.

Megan has always had an innate curiosity for the sciences. This curiosity has motivated her love for cooking and trying new recipes with her nana. Megan went to the University of Oregon where she was a student-athlete on the Acrobatics and Tumbling team. At Oregon, she founded Wishmakers on Campus, a student-run club to fundraise for Make-A-Wish Foundation Oregon. In 2019, Megan graduated from the Robert D. Clark's Honors College at the University of Oregon with her Bachelor of Science in Human Physiology and minors in Chemistry and Business Administration. Since then, she has moved back to Southern California so that she is close to her family while pursuing a Master of Science in Global Medicine. Megan is currently applying to medical schools and is pursuing a career in medicine.

Special cooking memories are shared by the authors, a nana and a granddaughter.

RECIPES

Aa Awesome Array of Animal Sandwiches

Bb Bold Blended Butter for One

Cc Crinkle, Crackle Corn on the Cob

Dd Delectable, Dainty Donuts

Ee Expressive Edible Eggheads

Ff Festive Fun Fudge

Gg Goddy-Goddy Guacamole

Hh Hunky-Dory Happy Cookies on a Stick

Ii Ideal Ice Cream Clowns

Jj Joyful, Jolly Message Cakes

Kk Krispie, Krispie Kudo Treats

Ll Laudable, Lickety-Split Lemonade Pie

Mm Mini Morsel Munchable Muffins

Nn Nifty, Nutty Nugget Bars

Oo Odd Ollie Octopus

Pp Pronto Pizza Pizazz

Qq Quirky, Quick Quesadilla Dogs

Rr Rip-Roaring Refreshing Rotini

Ss Sippy, Sippy Soda

Tt Tasty, Terrific Tostada Tidbits

Uu Unique Unicorn Horns

Vv Very Vibrant Vegetable Vittels

Ww Wild, Wild, Wheelies

Xx "X"hillarating "X"ample of an "X"

Yy Yummy, Yummy Yogurt Pops

Zz Zippy, Zany Zebra Sticks

ABC Chant

read as a rhythmic chant

ABCD won't you come and cook with me?
EFGHI we can make a lemonade pie.
JKL we'll follow the recipes very well!
MNO fun we'll have, so let's go.
QRS-TUV oh how happy we will be.
WXY and Z let's start cooking and you'll see.

-Catherine E. Montenegro

PARENTS AND TEACHERS

Countless numbers of primary teachers make collections of a variety of A B C books and use them in the classroom. This A B C book provides cooking opportunities with fun and engaging recipes to teach the following educational skills and safe use of kitchen tools.

SOCIAL SKILLS
working together
sharing

ART
Creativity
use of various colors,
shapes, lines

SENSORY EXPRESSION
Smell, taste, touch, sound, sight

SCIENCE
Observe physical
characteristics change
throughout cooking process

FINE MOTOR SKILLS
hand strength
hand-eye coordination:
stir, cut, whisk, roll, pat, chop, etc.

CLEANLINESS
wash hands
clean work area
use apron
use trash can

LANGUAGE ARTS
vocabulary development
sequencing
reading
listening
problem solving
following directions
writing a shopping list
learning capital and lowercase letters

MATH
measurement
fractions
counting
concept of time

Awesome Array of Animal Sandwiches

Aa

You need:

peanut butter
3 slices of toasted bread
animal cookie cutters

1. On each slice of toast, cut the same animal shape.
2. Spread peanut butter on one slice.
3. Put another slice on top.

4. Spread peanut butter on this slice.
5. Stand your animal sandwich up.
6. Enjoy it.

Bold Blended Butter for One

Bb

You need:

3 tbsp. whipping cream
1 small jar, chilled

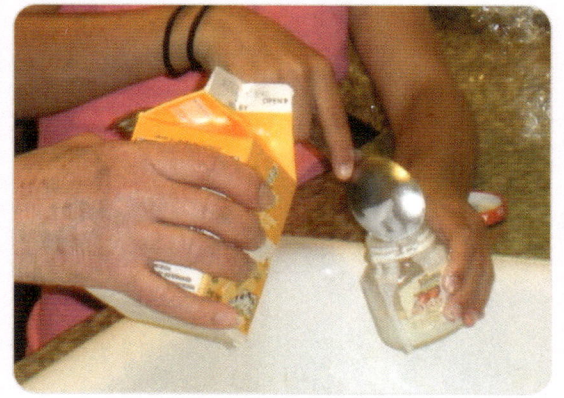 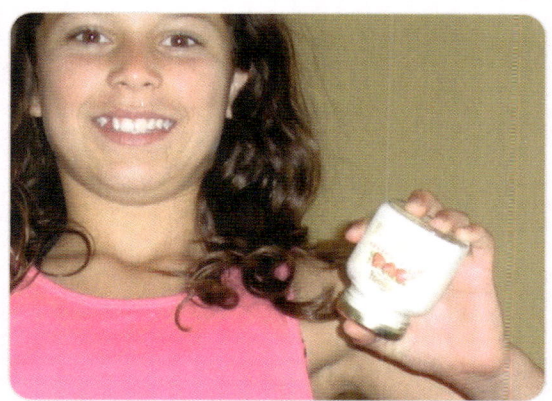 

1. Put the cream into the jar.
2. Put the lid on the jar.
3. Shake the jar for about 5 minutes until you see butter.

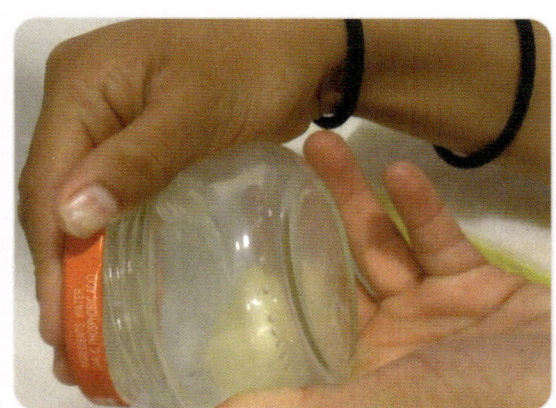  

4. Pour off the milk.
5. With a spoon, press the milk out of the butter and drain.
6. Enjoy on crackers, bread, or tortillas.

Crinkle, Crackle, Corn on the Cob

Cc

You need:

corn on the cob
butter
salt
waxed paper

Cooking Time:

2 ears: 4-5 mins
4 ears: 7-8 mins

1. Remove the husks and silk from the corn.
2. Rinse each corn.
3. Wrap each wet corn in a big square of waxed paper.

4. Twist each end of the wax paper closed.
5. Place the corn on a glass tray in the microwave oven.
6. Turn once during the cooking time.
7. Apply butter and salt sparingly.

Delectable Dainty Donuts

Dd

You need:

refrigerated biscuits
vegetable cooking oil
cinnamon sugar mixture

1. Separate the biscuits.
2. Poke a hole in the center of each biscuit.
3. Lightly brown the biscuits in a small amount of cooking oil.

4. Use tongs to turn the donuts over and brown the other side.
5. Place the donuts on a paper towel to soak up the excess oil.
6. Shake the warm donuts in a small paper bag of cinnamon sugar.
(or roll them in cinnamon sugar on a plate)

Expressive Eggheads

Ee

You need:

6 hard boiled eggs
1/2 tsp. of mustard
3 tbls. of mayonnaise
salt
black olives

1. Peel the chilled eggs.
2. Slice the eggs in half.
3. Carefully take out the yolks and put them into a bowl.
4. Break up the yolks with a fork.

5. Add the mustard and mayonnaise.
6. Mix.
7. Put the yolk mixture into the hollow of the white eggs.
8. Make expressive faces on the eggs with pieces of black olives.

Fun Festive Fudge

Ff

You need:

1 (18 oz.) pkg. of chocolate chips
1 can sweetened condensed milk
1 1/2 tsp. vanilla
3/4 c. chopped walnuts
1 pinch of salt

1. Butter an 8-inch square baking dish.
2. Mix the chocolate chips, sweetened condensed milk, and salt in a glass bowl.
3. Heat in the microwave for three 30 second intervals. Stir well between each interval.
4. Stir the mixture to make sure it is smooth.

5. Add vanilla and walnuts.
6. Stir until well mixed.
7. Put the mixture into an 8in x 8in glass dish.
8. Put into the refrigerator until firm (about 2.5 hours).
9. Cut into 1 inch squares and enjoy!

Goody-Goody Guacamole

Gg

You need:

1 ripe avocado (soft, but still firm when pressed)
1 green onion, chopped
1/8 tsp. ground garlic
1 tsp. chile salsa (optional)
salt to taste

1. Cut open the avocado.
2. Scrape the avocado into a bowl.
3. Mash the avocado.

4. Stir in the green onion, ground garlic, and salsa.
5. Add salt to taste.
6. Enjoy with tortilla chips.

Hunky-Dory Happy Cookies on a Stick

Hh

You need:

store bought sugar cookie dough
popsicle sticks
candy shapes

1. Cut 1/2 inch slices of the dough.
2. Roll each slice into a ball.
3. Place them on a cookie sheet.
4. Put a popsicle stick into each ball as seen in the picture.

5. Flatten each ball with the bottom of a glass.
6. Decorate them with candies to make a happy face.
7. Bake as directed on the package.

Ideal Ice Cream Clowns

Ii

You need:

ice cream
an ice cream scoop
a cone shaped ice cream cone
a can of whipped cream
small candies for: eyes, a nose, & a mouth

1. Make a rounded scoop of ice cream and place in a small bowl.
2. Put a cone on the ice cream to make a hat.
3. Use the candies to make a happy face with eyes, a nose and a mouth.

4. Use the whipped cream to make a ruffle collar on the clown.
5. Freeze until ready to serve.

Jolly, Joyful Message Cakes

You need:

cake mix
paper strips cut 3"x 1"
frosting   sprinkles   muffin pan

1. Write jolly messages on the paper strips and fold them.
Examples: "You are nice." "I like you." "You are my friend."
2. Make the cake mix as directed.

3. Fill the cones 3/4 full with the cake mix.
4. Put the cones in muffin pans or a cake pan.
5. Poke the jolly messages into the cake batter in the cones.
6. Bake at 350 degrees for 18 to 20 minutes.
7. When cooled, frost with a colorful store bought frosting.
PS: Don't eat the paper.

Krispie, Krispie Kudos Treats

You need:

6 cups rice cereal
1 package of mini marshmallows
1 cup peanut butter chips
2 cups of chocolate chips
1/2 stick of butter
waxed paper
9x13 inch pan

1. Butter and line the 9x13 pan with waxed paper.
2. Put the rice cereal in the 9x13.
3. Melt the butter in a medium sized bowl.
4. Mix the marshmallows in with the melted butter.
5. Microwave the butter and marshmallows for 1 minute. Mix.

6. Pour melted marshmallows into the 9x13 on top of the rice cereal.
7. Mix with your hands until all cereal is coated with melted marshmallow. Push down into the pan.
8. Melt the chocolate chips and peanut butter chips.
9. Pour melted chocolate and peanut butter chips on top of the rice cereal.
10. Put into refrigerator until chocolate peanut butter topping is firm. Let sit 30 mins before serving.

Laudable, Lickety-split Lemonade Pie

Ll

You need:

six oz. can of frozen lemonade
1 fourteen oz. can of
sweetened condensed milk
a chocolate pie crust
1 eight oz. carton of whip topping

1. Mix.
1 six oz. can of frozen lemonade or 1/2 of a 12 oz. can
1 fourteen oz. can of sweetened condensed milk

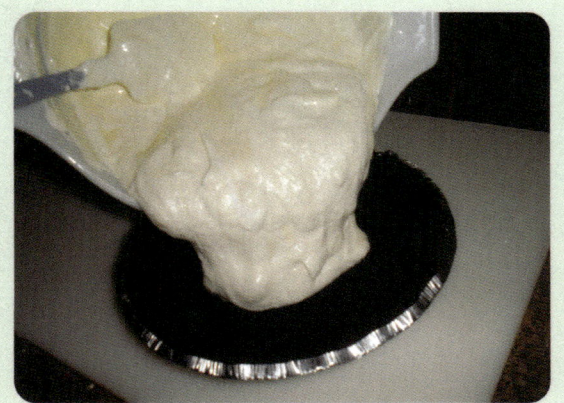  

2. Fold in: 1 eight oz. carton of whip topping
3. Pour into a chocolate pie crust.
4. Freeze about 3 hours.

Mini Morsel Munchable Muffins

Mm

You need:
blueberries
mini muffin pan
2 cups all purpose flour
2 tsp. baking powder
1/2 cup unsalted butter softened
1 cup granulated sugar
2 eggs
1 tsp. vanilla extract
1/2 cup whole milk

1. Preheat the oven to 375 degrees.
2. Line a 24 count mini muffin pan with mini muffin papers.
3. Combine the flour and the baking powder.
4. Beat the butter and sugar together.
5. Add the eggs one at a time and mix well
6. Add the vanilla and the flour. Then mix.

7. Add the milk. Mix until the batter is smooth.
8. Mix in the blueberries.
9. Pour the batter into each muffin paper.
10. Place the pan into the oven and bake for 17-20 minutes until the muffins are slightly golden brown on top.
11. Let cool for 5 minutes. Then transfer to a wire rack.

Nifty, Nutty Nugget Bars

Nn

You need:

12 oz. of chocolate chips
6 oz. of butterscotch chips
1 cup peanut butter
1 package of small marshmallows
1 cup of Spanish peanuts
a 9x13 pan

1. Melt together:
The chocolate and butterscotch chips

2. Add:
the cup of peanut butter
the package of small marshmallows
the cup of Spanish peanuts

3. Put in a 9x13 pan
and refrigerate.

4. When it is firm,
cut into bars.

Odd Ollie Octopus

O o

You need:

**hot dogs
plastic knife
candy circles for eyes**

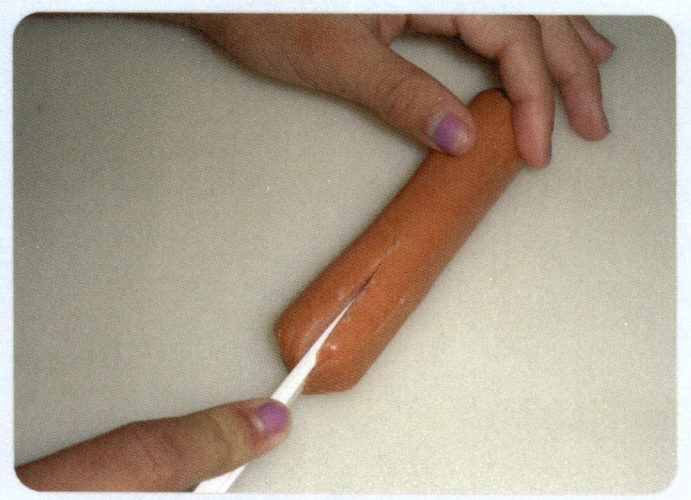 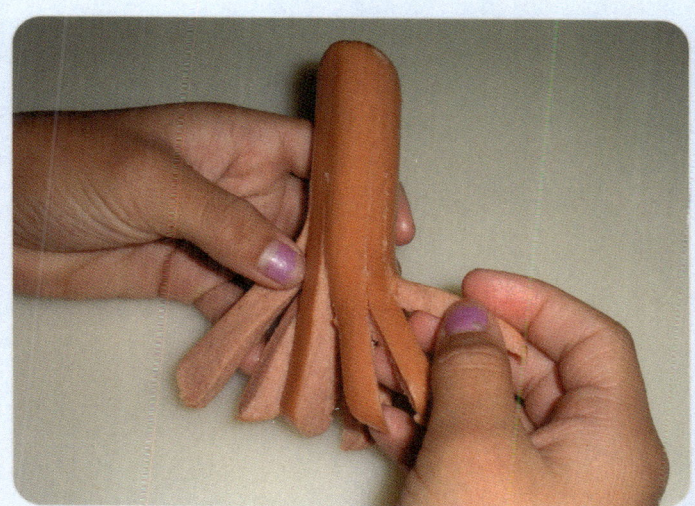

1. Cook hot dog in the microwave. Cook about 15 seconds.
2. Slice the hot dog into 8 legs (about half way up).

3. Use mustard to stick on the candy eyes.
4. Have fun nibbling on Ollie.

Pronto Pizza Pizazz

Pp

You need:
English muffins
spaghetti sauce
mozzarella cheese
toppings of your choice
(pepperoni, veggies)

1. Put a thin layer of sauce on 1/2 of a muffin.
2. Put on pieces of the mozzarella cheese.

3. Put on your toppings.
4. Microwave for 1 minute.

Quirky, Quick Quesadilla Dogs

Qq

You need:

small flour tortillas
hot dogs
mustard and ketchup
toothpicks

1. Wrap a tortilla around a hot dog.
2. Use a toothpick to close the tortilla.
3. Microwave it for 1 minute.

4. Remove with a hot pad.
5. Use mustard or ketchup as a dipping sauce.

Rip Roaring Refreshing Rotini

Rr

You need:

1 pound cooked rotini pasta
3 chopped green onions
1 zucchini, sliced
1 yellow squash, sliced
2 cups grape tomatoes cut in half
garlic powder to taste
1/2 cup parmesan cheese
red chile flakes (optional)
olive oil

1. Cook onions, zucchini, and squash in olive oil for 3 minutes.
2. Add tomatoes and cook 4 minutes.
3. Add salt and garlic powder to taste.
4. Add two shakes of chile flakes (optional).

5. Mix in the drained pasta.
6. Mix in 2 tbls. of olive oil.
7. Put mixture in a casserole dish.
8. Top with parmesan cheese.

Sippy, Sippy Soda

Ss

You need:

oranges
a large glass
1 cup sparkling water
a plastic knife
a juicer
1/2 tsp. of sugar

1. On a flat surface, roll an orange under your hand.
2. Cut the orange in half.
3. Squeeze the orange with the juicer.
4. Pour the juice into a tall glass. Add the sugar.

5. Put 2/3 cup sparkling water into the glass.
6. Stir.
You can make lemonade this same way.

Tasty, Terrific Tostada Tidbits

Tt

You need:

round corn tortilla chips
refried beans
cheddar cheese slices cut into 4 squares
lettuce pieces
tomato slices
avocado slices

  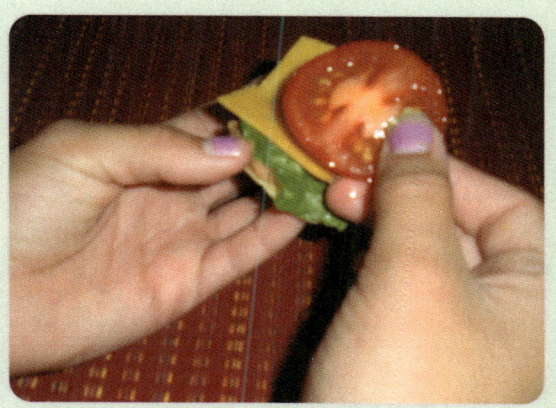

1. Spread a thin layer of beans on the chips
2. Place lettuce on the beans.
3. Place a cheese square on next.

4. Put a tomato slice on next.
5. Put the avocado on top.
Enjoy!

Unique Unicorn Horns

You need:

mini waffle cones
cut fruits of your choice
peanut butter
whipped cream

1. Stuff the cones with cut fruit.
2. Peanut butter is good.
3. Top with whipped cream.

Very Vibrant Vegetable Vittels

Vv

You need:

1/3 cup dry buttermilk
2 tbs. dried parsley
2 tsp. dried dill weed
1 tsp. garlic powder
1 tsp. onion powder
2 tsp. dried onion flakes
1 tsp. pepper
1 tsp. dried chives
1 1/2 tsp. salt
1 cup of sour cream
several vegetables of your choice,
such as: broccoli - carrots
celery stalks - grape tomatoes

1. Combine dry ingredients.
2. Stir dry ingredients into 1 cup of sour cream.
3. Refrigerate homemade ranch until ready to serve.
4. Wash the vegetables

5. Pat them dry
6. Group the vegetables into a divided dish and serve with ranch.

Wild, Wild Wheelies

Ww

You need:

small flour tortillas
8 oz. cream cheese
2 tbs. ranch salad dressing
1 green onion chopped
2 thin slices of deli ham
1 slice of cheddar cheese

1. Soften cream cheese.
2. Mix cream cheese, salad dressing, and onion.
3. Spread a thin layer of the mixture on a tortilla.
4. Layer the ham and cheese on the tortilla.
5. Start on one side of the tortilla and roll it up.

6. Wrap each each rolled up tortilla in plastic wrap.
7. Put in the refrigerator for one or two hours.
8. Unwrap the tortillas and cut.
9. Slice "wheelie" slices and serve.

"X"llerating" "X"Ample of an "X"

Xx

You need:

**refrigerator biscuit dough
a topping**

1. Form the letter X with pieces of the biscuit dough.
2. Bake as directed on the package.
3. Cool the letters.
4. Spread a topping on the letters.
Ideas: butter - cream cheese - jelly - peanut butter

Yummy, Yummy Yogurt Pops

Yy

You need:

2 cups of vanilla yogurt
1-1/2 cups orange juice
small 3 oz. paper cups
popsicle sticks or plastic spoons

1. Mix yogurt and orange juice together.
2. Pour mixture into the small paper cups.
3. Place the sticks or spoons into the cups.

4. Freeze them.
5. Remove cups as shown in the photo.
6. Enjoy!

Zippy, Zany Zebra Sticks

Zz

You need:

celery stalks
black olives
cream cheese

1. Wash the celery stalks and pat them dry.
2. Spread cream cheese on each piece.
3. Cut the olives into small slices.
4. Place the olives on the celery to look like zebra stripes.

CPSIA information can be obtained at www.ICGtesting.com
Printed in the USA
BVIW122332050420
576897BV00035B/648